The Story of America

THE BRITISH COLONIES

By M. Alexander Harasymiw

Gareth Stevens
Publishing

Please visit our Web site, www.garethstevens.com. For a free color catalog of all our high-quality books, call toll free 1-800-542-2595 or fax 1-877-542-2596.

Library of Congress Cataloging-in-Publication Data

Harasymiw, M. Alexander.
 The British colonies / M. Alexander Harasymiw.
     p. cm. – (The story of America)
 Includes index.
 ISBN 978-1-4339-4765-0 (pbk.)
 ISBN 978-1-4339-4766-7 (6-pack)
 ISBN 978-1-4339-4764-3 (library binding)
 1. United States—History—Colonial period, ca. 1600–1775—Juvenile literature. I. Title.
 E188.H27 2011
 973.2–dc22

                                    2010036597

First Edition

Published in 2011 by
Gareth Stevens Publishing
111 East 14th Street, Suite 349
New York, NY 10003

Copyright © 2011 Gareth Stevens Publishing

Designer: Daniel Hosek
Editor: Therese Shea

Photo credits: Cover, pp. 1, 8, 9, 21, 22–23, 27 MPI/Getty Images; p. 4 Shutterstock.com; p. 5 Apic/Hulton Archive/Getty Images; p. 6 Fotosearch/Getty Images; pp. 10–11 Lambert/ Getty Images; pp. 12, 19 Stock Montage/Getty Images; pp. 14–15, 17, 18, 25, 29 Hulton Archive/Getty Images; p. 24 Getty Images.

Printed in the United States of America

CPSIA compliance information: Batch #CW11GS: For further information contact Gareth Stevens, New York, New York at 1-800-542-2595.

Contents

Words in the glossary appear in **bold** type the first time they are used in the text.

The Europeans Arrive

Europeans weren't the first people to come to America. Native Americans had been there for thousands of years. However, since Europeans didn't know the Americas existed, it seemed an amazing discovery to them. Europeans began exploring this "New World" at the end of the 1400s. One of the most famous early explorers was Christopher Columbus, who sailed for Spain. Many early explorers were interested in finding riches. Other **expeditions** traveled to trade with Native Americans. Still others, for a variety of reasons, sought to make this new land their home. The most successful settlers were the British. They governed the 13 colonies that became the foundation of the United States of America.

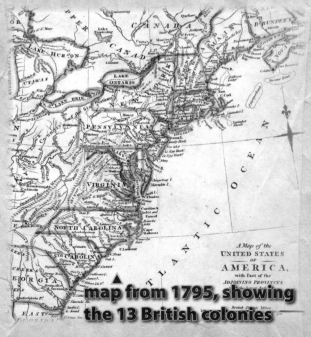

map from 1795, showing the 13 British colonies

Christopher Columbus (center) has long been called the "discoverer" of the New World. However, Vikings had visited North America 500 years earlier.

DID YOU KNOW?

The first permanent European settlement in North America was St. Augustine, Florida, which was settled in 1565 by the Spanish.

A Mystery on Roanoke Island

The first British attempt to build a permanent settlement in North America was in 1587. About 117 people settled on Roanoke Island in present-day North Carolina. After a time, the new settlement needed supplies. They waited, but no ships came. Finally, the governor of the island—John White— sailed to England for supplies. Conflicts between Spain and England kept White from returning immediately. He was delayed several years.

When he returned, the word "Croatoan" was John White's only clue about what happened to the Roanoke Island settlers.

When White finally arrived back on Roanoke Island in 1591, there was no sign of the colonists. All that remained was a mysterious message carved into a tree near the settlement. White couldn't search long because bad weather forced his ships to return to England. No one knows for sure what happened to the colonists of Roanoke Island.

Croatoan

The mysterious message carved into a tree on Roanoke Island said "Croatoan." Some think it was meant to tell John White that the colonists had moved to nearby Croatoan Island. "Croatoan" may have also referred to the Croatoan Indians. However, White couldn't locate the settlers, and the mystery has never been solved. Modern Lumbee Indians believe they're the descendants of the colonists and Indians who lived near them.

Virginia

Roanoke Island ▶

North Carolina

South Carolina

DID YOU KNOW?

The first English baby born in North America was named Virginia Dare. She was born on Roanoke Island in 1587.

First Permanent Settlement

In 1607, about 100 settlers from England arrived in the Virginia colony and founded Jamestown. Jamestown was the first lasting British settlement in North America. Initially, the colonists looked for gold. They didn't spend much time growing food or even searching for it. In the first years of the Jamestown settlement, almost half the colonists died as a result of hunger, disease, and battles with Native Americans.

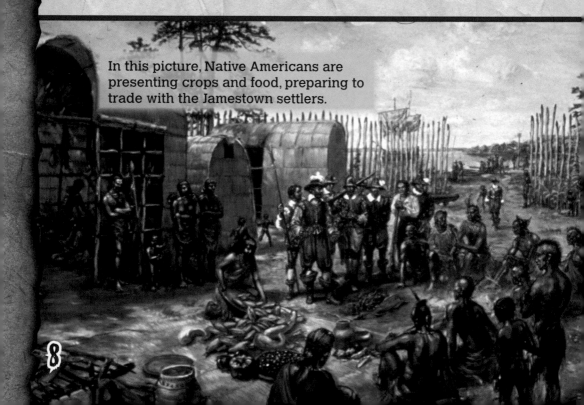

In this picture, Native Americans are presenting crops and food, preparing to trade with the Jamestown settlers.

However, Jamestown didn't disappear like the settlement on Roanoke Island. It was able to succeed with the help of the Powhatan Indians and provisions arriving by boat. The colonists of Jamestown were able to pay for the supplies from England by growing tobacco and selling it to people in England.

DID YOU KNOW?

Jamestown leader John Smith was captured by Opechancanough, a Powhatan who had been kidnapped and sent to Spain in 1559. He returned to North America in the 1570s.

The Real Pocahontas

Pocahontas was the daughter of Powhatan, the chief of a Native American tribe near Jamestown. Powhatan's tribe captured the leader of Jamestown, John Smith, when he went to trade with them. According to a story Smith told years later, Pocahontas kept the tribe from killing him. The story may not be true, but Pocahontas was a friend to the settlers. She married settler John Rolfe in 1614. She was renamed Lady Rebecca and traveled to England with her husband in 1616. She died there in 1617.

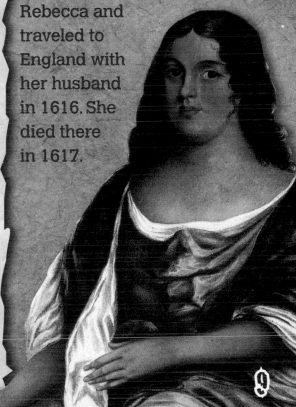

Pocahontas ▶

Reasons for Colonizing

People had many reasons for settling in the British colonies of North America. Religion was one motive to start a new life in a new place. In the late 1500s, a group of people called Puritans became unhappy with the Protestant church in England. By 1620, some Puritans had settled in the British colonies in order to practice their faith the way they wanted.

Puritans took special care and interest in educating their children, the future leaders of their church.

People came from other countries for religious reasons as well. Protestants from France, known as Huguenots, settled in the British colonies to escape religious **persecution** in their country. Many Germans settled in the British colonies to flee the Thirty Years' War, a conflict between Catholics and Protestants in Germany.

The Pilgrims

Initially called "Old Comers," the settlers of Plymouth, Massachusetts, were later known as Pilgrims. About one-third of the settlers were a group of Puritans known as Separatists. Unlike most Puritans who wanted to "purify" the Church of England, the Separatists formed a new church. The Separatists among the Pilgrims had left England and settled in Holland. However, they came to feel that they would lose their British identity if they remained. They decided to move to the British colonies.

DID YOU KNOW?

The Pilgrims originally intended on settling in the Virginia colony. Because of bad weather, they landed at Plymouth, Massachusetts, and decided to stay.

Many people came to America in search of wealth. Colonists acquired land, grew crops, and raised animals. The original inhabitants—the Native Americans—were often driven away, killed, or died from diseases brought by the new settlers.

Trading posts such as this one were places for all kinds of settlers and Native Americans to trade and purchase supplies.

As the colonies grew, they became an important part of the British Empire. The colonies provided supplies to England and in return bought British goods. The New England colonies in the North—Massachusetts, New Hampshire, Rhode Island, and Connecticut—sold fish and whale oil to Europe. New England trees were used as lumber for shipbuilding. Colonists from the middle colonies—New York, New Jersey, Pennsylvania, and Delaware—sold animal furs and crops such as corn and wheat. In the southern colonies—Virginia, Maryland, North Carolina, South Carolina, and Georgia—the valuable crops were tobacco, rice, and **indigo**.

Trade Routes

In addition to the trade route between the British colonies and Europe, there were other well-traveled trade routes. One was called the "triangular trade" route. Slaves were taken from Africa to sugar plantations in the Caribbean. Then **molasses** was taken from the Caribbean sugar plantations to North America. The molasses was used to make rum that was then shipped to Africa to help purchase new slaves.

DID YOU KNOW?

Since money was scarce in the colonies, people were sometimes paid with tobacco.

Before the rise of slavery, indentured servants worked on large farms and plantations in the British colonies.

Hardships brought some Europeans to the British North American colonies. Many people arrived as **indentured servants**. In the early days of the colonies, workers were in short supply. Europeans who couldn't afford the cost of the trip could enter into a contract with a colonist. The colonist would pay the cost of a person's voyage to America. In return, the traveler would agree to be an indentured servant, usually for a period of 4 to 7 years.

Unwilling Colonists

The number of indentured servants coming to America didn't satisfy the need for workers in the colonies. England passed a law stating that any criminal sentenced to death could instead be sentenced to work in the colonies. Other unwilling colonists were actually kidnap victims! The practice of kidnapping children and forcing them into servitude was called "spiriting."

Some people in the colonies preferred having indentured servants to hiring other colonists. Indentured servants were required by law to work, whereas other colonists could leave the job when they wanted. Some indentured servants were treated poorly, like slaves. Others were given money or land when their years of work were done.

DID YOU KNOW?

Some indentured servants' contracts promised rewards at the end of service, such as guns, cattle, land, crops, and clothes.

In 1619, the first black African slaves came to Virginia. At first, they were treated as indentured servants. Until the early 1700s, the number of willing and unwilling workers coming from Europe was enough to meet labor needs. In fact, white servants were less expensive than purchasing slaves. Eventually, the colonies needed more workers than Europe could provide. The number of African slaves greatly increased. Many slaves were sent to the South, where they worked on plantations growing tobacco and rice.

Slaves didn't have the rights that indentured servants had. They had to work for as long as their owner wanted. They could be bought and sold. They couldn't take their owners to court for treating them cruelly.

The Stono Slave Rebellion

Occasionally, slaves revolted against their owners. On September 9, 1739, slaves in South Carolina broke into a warehouse containing guns. They killed several people who had treated them badly. They spared those who had been kind. Soon, the slaves were attacked and defeated by the local **militia**. In total, about 40 slaves and 20 other people were killed in what was called the Stono **Rebellion**.

DID YOU KNOW?

In 1663, a court in Virginia decided that a child born to a slave was also a slave.

Many families were torn apart by the institution of slavery. Here, Dutch sailors present slaves to the colonists.

Education

As colonists had families, there was a growing need to educate children. At first, children were taught at home. Then, the colony of Massachusetts ordered the establishment of the first public schools. These schools were supported financially by their communities. Students were taught to read and write. They also learned Latin, Greek, and other subjects. Schools were attended mostly by boys. If girls went to school, it was only for a few years.

Harvard University, shown here around 1770, was named after minister John Harvard, who donated many books to the school.

As religion was an important part of colonial life, especially in the New England colonies, the first colleges were set up to train clergy. These were called divinity schools. Wealthy students interested in pursuing other professions, such as law or medicine, usually returned to England to study.

DID YOU KNOW?

The first school of higher learning in America was Harvard University, started in Boston in 1636.

Reading

Religious book collections were common in the colonies. Medical books helped colonists treat sicknesses, since there were few doctors. Eventually, libraries were established. Benjamin Franklin started the first lending library in the colonies in 1731.

Newspapers were popular in the colonies, too. First printed in 1704, the *Boston News-Letter* was the first continuously publishing colonial newspaper. Newspapers were a source of information from other colonies as well as from England.

◀ Benjamin Franklin

Colonial Governments

At the beginning of the colonial period, the British government allowed the colonies a great amount of self-governance. One reason for this was that several early colonies were established by businesses. British companies obtained permission to settle certain parts of America without interference from other businesses. For example, the Virginia Company of London (also called the London Company) was given a **charter** in 1606 to found settlements on the eastern coast of North America. The colony of Jamestown, Virginia, resulted from this. Other colonies, such as Pennsylvania, were given to subjects of the British king to pay off debts.

After a colony was established, a governor was appointed with the power to select officials and to suggest and revoke laws. The British ruler and his appointed officials reserved the right to change these laws.

The Thirteenth Colony

James Edward Oglethorpe was a British official who wanted to find a home in America for imprisoned debtors of "good moral character." At the time, people were put in prison if they couldn't pay back money they owed. In 1732, Oglethorpe received a charter to colonize land between the Savannah and Altamaha Rivers. Oglethorpe founded the colony of Georgia in 1733, naming it for King George II, and governed it until 1743. Oglethorpe lived to see Georgia become part of the United States.

James Edward Oglethorpe

THE BRITISH COLONIES

Colony Name	Year Founded	Founded By
Virginia	1607	Virginia Company of London
Massachusetts	1620	Pilgrims
New Hampshire	1623	David Thomson
New York	1624	Dutch West India Company (England takes control in 1664)
Connecticut	1633	Thomas Hooker
Maryland	1634	Lord Baltimore
Rhode Island	1636	Roger Williams
Delaware	1638	New Sweden Company (England takes control in 1664)
Pennsylvania	1643	New Sweden Company (William Penn granted control by English king in 1681)
North Carolina	around 1650	settlers from Virginia
New Jersey	1660	Dutch West India Company (British nobles take control in 1664)
South Carolina	1670	British nobles with a royal charter
Georgia	1733	James Edward Oglethorpe

Each colony had a lawmaking assembly. Nearly all the assemblies were composed of two bodies. The upper house was appointed by the colonial governor to serve as his advisers. The lower house was a representative body of the colony elected by voters. Usually this lower house made the local laws.

Distance made colonial governments necessary. During the colonial period, the only way to travel across the Atlantic Ocean was by boat. The trip

between England and the British colonies took 8 to 12 weeks, so even the simplest communication was very slow. A colonist might have waited 6 months to receive a letter! It was difficult and expensive to make any but the biggest decisions in England.

The House of Burgesses, shown here, inspired other colonies to create similar governments.

The House of Burgesses

The first British colonial representative assembly was the House of Burgesses. It was formed in 1619 in Jamestown. The House of Burgesses was composed of two elected representatives from each settlement in the growing Virginia colony. These 22 men had the power to make laws, collect taxes, and pay for public building projects.

Relationships with Natives

Native Americans regarded the colonists warily. In some regions, they viewed the colonists as a threat and attacked. In other places, Native Americans were more accepting. They helped the colonists adjust to life on the new continent. They showed colonists how to raise corn and other crops, and where to fish and hunt. The colonists provided goods Native Americans

Samoset, an Abenaki Indian, greets the Plymouth settlers, offering the friendship and help of his people.

couldn't make, such as guns, gunpowder, and metal tools.

However, good relations became strained as the number of colonists grew. They moved deeper into Native American lands. There were several wars between the colonists and Native Americans throughout the colonial period. Native Americans were eventually forced out of the British colonies. Diseases brought by colonists killed millions of Native Americans.

DID YOU KNOW?

The Native American population of Virginia dropped from about 50,000 when the colonists arrived in the early 17th century to about 3,000 in 1670.

King Philip's War

Metacom, called King Philip by the colonists, was the leader of the Wampanoag tribe of southern New England. The growing population of British colonists and their movement onto Native American land angered Metacom. In 1675, the hanging of several Native Americans at Plymouth—including Metacom's brother—sparked the beginning of King Philip's War. The war was fought throughout present-day Connecticut, Rhode Island, and Massachusetts. Both sides raided towns and villages. The war ended in August 1676 with Metacom's capture and death.

◄ Metacom

Other European Powers

England was only one of the numerous European countries to settle North America. The Spanish settlements were mainly to the west of the British colonies as well as south in what is now Florida. The French settled in large numbers in present-day Canada and along the Mississippi River. The French were a big presence in the current state of Louisiana. The Dutch settled along the Hudson River in what would become New York. The biggest Dutch settlements were New Amsterdam, which later became New York City, and Fort Orange, which became Albany.

The Dutch colonies became English possessions in 1664, after the governor of New Amsterdam surrendered without a fight. The French almost totally disappeared as a result of the French and Indian War. The Spanish presence in North America didn't end until the 1800s.

The French and Indian War

The largest war between England and France in North America—known as the French and Indian War—began in 1755. Both sides had support from Native American **allies**. The British were eventually able to block communication between France and their North American colonies. This, along with the capture of Montreal in Canada, led to the Treaty of Paris in 1763. France surrendered all land in North America except the city of New Orleans.

A French officer raises his arm to signal the attack on British-held Fort Duquesne in Pennsylvania during the French and Indian War.

DID YOU KNOW?

Sweden had a presence in North America, too. In 1638, the New Sweden Company founded a colony in what is now Delaware. In 1643, they founded another in Pennsylvania.

Road to War

    With the defeat of the French and their Native American allies following the French and Indian War, the French were no longer a danger to the colonies. The British wanted their colonists to pay for the colonial governments and defense against other threats. The British taxed them to raise the money, which angered the colonists. In 1763, a British **proclamation** was handed down that said colonists could no longer settle lands west of the Appalachian Mountains. The land was reserved for the Native Americans. The proclamation was also meant to keep colonists and Native Americans safe from each other. Colonists quickly disregarded the order.

Timeline

1587
Settlers arrive on Roanoke Island

1607
Settlers arrive in Jamestown

1619
House of Burgesses formed in Jamestown

1619
First African slaves arrive in Virginia

1620
Pilgrims settle Plymouth

1636
Harvard University founded

By the 1770s, many American colonists wanted complete self-rule. The American Revolution was about to begin.

In 1775, the first shots of the American Revolution were fired in Lexington, Massachusetts.

1664
The Netherlands surrenders New Netherland to England

1675
King Philip's War begins

1676
Death of Metacom and the end of King Philip's War

1739
Stono Rebellion breaks out in South Carolina

1763
French and Indian War ends with the Treaty of Paris

1776
British colonies declare independence

Glossary

ally: one of two or more people or groups who work together

charter: an official agreement giving permission to do something

expedition: a trip made for a certain purpose

indentured servant: an individual who signs a contract agreeing to work for a set period of time in exchange for money or other benefits

indigo: a plant with spikes of red or purple flowers, or the blue dye that comes from it

militia: a military force composed of citizens, used in emergencies

molasses: a gooey brown liquid that is produced while making sugar

persecution: making a group of people suffer cruel or unfair treatment

proclamation: a public announcement

rebellion: a fight to overthrow a government

For More Information

BOOKS

George, Lynn. *What Do You Know About Colonial America?* New York, NY: Rosen Publishing Group, 2008.

Huey, Lois Miner. *American Archaeology Uncovers the Earlicst English Colonies.* New York, NY: Marshall Cavendish Benchmark, 2010.

Roberts, Russell. *Life in Colonial America.* Hockessin, DE: Mitchell Lane Publishers, 2008.

WEB SITES

America in the British Empire
www.history.com/topics/america-in-the-british-empire
Check out videos and photo collections about many topics involving colonial times.

Daily Life in the Colonies
www.pbs.org/ktca/liberty/perspectives_daily.html
Learn about many aspects of everyday life in the New England colonies.

Index